Unabashedly Bold

Unabashedly Bold

Suzi Tetz Weaver

Copyright © 2025, Suzi Tetz Weaver
All rights reserved. Printed in the U.S.A.

No part of this publication may be reproduced or transmitted in any form or by any means, electronic or mechanical, including photocopy, recording or any information storage and retrieval system now known or to be invented, without permission in writing from the publisher, except by a reviewer who wishes to quote brief passages in connection with a review written for inclusion in a magazine, newspaper or broadcast.

Quantity Purchases:
Companies, professional groups, clubs, and other organizations may qualify for special terms when ordering quantities of this title.
For information, email info@ebooks2go.net, or call (847) 598-1150 ext. 4141.
www.ebooks2go.net

Published in the United States by eBooks2go, Inc.
1827 Walden Office Square, Suite 260,
Schaumburg, IL 60173

ISBN: 978-1-5457-6080-2

Library of Congress Cataloging in Publication

This Book Belongs to My Beautiful Friend

Gifted with Gratitude for You by

Dedication......................

We Dedicate this Journey to Our Sister in Christ Beautiful Beverly Jo Gerlitz, Who has been an Amazing Friend, Soul Sister, Prayer Partner, Trusted Confidant, and Life Saver!

Beverly is my Sister both by Blood & in Christ. She Prayed for me for 21 Years Until I got Saved, which I will be Eternally Grateful for! She is The Best Friend & The Best Sister I could ever Hope & Pray for! Beverly is Beautiful Inside & Out from the Top of her Head to the Tip of her Toes. She has such a Humble Heart of Compassion for all!

She has been such an Inspiration, Trusted Confidant, Encourager, Spiritual Mentor, Woman after Gods Heart, and Powerful Princess Prayer Warrior for the Kingdom of Heaven!

Beverly introduced Brenda & I and I am so Grateful that she did. Brenda has been such a Blessing to Us Both! Brenda has also been a Trusted Friend, Spiritual Mentor & Powerful Princess Prayer Warrior Partner for Us. Beverly & I consider Brenda a Soul Sister & an Amazing Inspiration in her Spiritual Walk. Beautiful Brenda, May You be Abundantly Blessed & Highly Favored by Our King of Kings Jesus!!!

Unabashedly Bold.......

Author is Suzi Tetz-Weaver Who is a Prophetic Voice Who Receives Words from Holy Spirit to Inspire & Encourage Women!

Creative Director is Brenda Bonin Who Walks by His Word & Prophesizes Over Others Holy Spirit puts on her Heart!

Table of Contents

1. Unabashedly Bold iii
2. Dedication Letter vi
3. Author Suzi Weaver/Creative Director Brenda Bonin 1
4. Intro Letter 3
5. Join Us on a 7-week journey 4
6. Unabashedly Word Description 4
7. For each Chapter in order: 1. Worship Songs to Play or Sing. 2. What each letter stands for with Scripture. 3. Poem. 4. Questions for Reflection. 5. One Blank page to write on. 6. Ending Prayer. 7. Discussion. 14
8. Suzi Salvation Story is Whispers 59
9. Prayer to Accept Christ 61

Invitation Letter.......

Dear Sisters,

We want you to know how much you are valued. Our King of Kings, Jesus, absolutely adores you. Do yourself a favor and let Him into your heart today.

With just a simple prayer asking Jesus to forgive you of any of your sins, knowingly or unknowingly, confess with your mouth that He died on the cross for you & rose from the grave, and believe this with your whole heart. Invite Jesus into your life and you will be amazed at all the blessings He will bestow upon you.

Welcome to His Royal Kingdom where His will is done on Earth as it is in Heaven!

Lovingly from Your Sisters in Christ,

Brenda & Suzi

Deuteronomy 14:2 "For you are a people holy to the Lord your God, and the Lord has chosen you to be a people for His treasured possession, out of all the peoples who are on the face of the earth."

Join Us on a Seven-Week Journey Toward becoming Unabashedly Bold!

Outline for Individual, Partner, or Small Groups

1. Welcome & Introduce All Attending
2. Start with Prayer, Worship & Intro Letter
3. Week One = All Pages from Letters U-A
4. Week Two = All Pages from Letters B-S
5. Week Three = All Pages from Letters H&E
6. Week Four = All Pages for Letters D-Y
7. Week Five = All Pages for Letters B&O
8. Week Six = All Pages for Letters L&D
9. Week Seven = Self or Group Reflections

Unabashedly Bold intro Letter explanation:

Unabashedly Bold = (To have Shameless Courage)

Unabashedly Synonyms:
Brazen/Shameless/Unblushing/
Courtesy/Respect/Right/Unintimidated/
Unembarrassed/Unashamed/Unapologetic/
Undisguised/Gleeful/Certain

Bold Synonyms:
Courageous/Brave/Daring/Fearless/Audacious/
Dashing/Gallant/Unflinching/Confident/
Spirited/Positive/Assured/Undaunted/Unafraid/
Valiant/Adventuresome/Enterprising

Worship Songs for Lesson #1 Letters U-A:

1. "Tremble" by Lauren Daigle
2. "Still on the Trone" by Paul Daughtery
3. "Courageous" by Casting Crowns

U is for Unabashedly

2 Timothy 3:17 "That the woman of God may be competent, equipped for every good work."

Unabashedly is having total confidence without compromise. You see, Unabashedly Bold means to have Unapologetic Confidence, which we get from Our One & Only Savior Jesus Christ. To Stand firm on His Rock & His Word without wavering whatsoever!

Prayer for Unabashedly,

Abba Father, Thank You that I know I can depend on You to be Unabashedly Bold while I Cling to Our Relationship & Stand on Your Word. Help me to Confidently Share Your Love with others!

In the Confident name of Jesus, Amen.

"Unabashedly Bold"

Women of Wonder Praising Our Lord Divine.

Invading their atmosphere in His perfect Time.

Women He Wonderfully & Fashionably Made.

God was Pleased when upon her His eyes He did Gaze.

An Amazing Creation full of Beauty & Grace.

Beautifully Decorating her with Colored Eyes Placed upon her Delicate Face.

Soft Kissable Lips & Shiny Wavy Tresses.

Delicately framing her with a Desirable Figure under Chiffon Dresses.

Creating inside her a Child & Bringing it to Life.

As she lay joined with her Husband, as his Adored Wife.

Full of Compassion with a Heart made of Gold.

God Creating Woman was Unabashedly Bold!

Inspired & Written by Your Sister in Christ, Suzi Weaver who lives to be Unabashedly Bold!!!

Questions for the Letter U for Unabashedly

1. What makes you feel Unabashedly confident?
2. What do you do to help you feel confident?
3. What feelings do you have when you are confident?
4. When you are confident how do you act compared to when you aren't confident?
5. What can you do to instill confidence while witnessing to others?
6. What can you do to help instill confidence in others?
7. What Sisters in Christ would you choose to be confidence partners?

N is for New Creation in Christ

2 Corinthians 5:17 "Therefore, if anyone is in Christ, they are a new creation & the old one is gone. The old has gone, the new is here."

Once we Accept Jesus Christ in Our Heart to be Our Only Savior He renews Our Mind, Heart, Body & Soul. Our Spirit Comes Alive in Him. Daily, we must Take Up our Cross & Follow Him. Keep His Word in Our Mind & Heart so He can Truly Transform Us from the Inside Out.

Prayer for New Creation in Christ,

Sweet Son Jesus, I am so eternally grateful for my Salvation through You. Please help me to daily renew my Mind in You & Keep Your Word Fresh on my Lips.

I Adore my Relationship with You, so please block anyone or anything in my Life that would hinder it & is Not of You!

In the Sweet name of Jesus, Amen.

"Ideal Identity"

Ideal identity should be established in Christ,
That is what it is all about.
Know His infinite love for you, never should you doubt.
Open your heart to let all His love in.
He cleanses you with Jesus's blood, He cleanses all your sin.
Break down those walls of bondage
Break those chains around your heart.
Graciously receive His love, in you, He will impart.
Abba, Father, Friend, and Judge, He loves us all so much.
Be open to His Favor, Grace, and Mercy, His Tender Loving Touch.
Did your earthly Daddy show his love for you?
Your value and your worth?
Your Daddy in Heaven's Love is so much greater
Than the one on this fallen earth.
Looking for God in all the wrong churches.
Looking for love in the wrong man.
I see now on Christ I Forever will Stand!
Written by Suzi Weaver.

Questions for Letter N = New in Christ

1. What exactly does "New in Christ" mean to you?
2. What do you do to "Renew Your Mind in Christ" on a daily basis?
3. Do you feel you are "Taking every thought Captive?"
4. If yes, how do you do take every thought captive?
5. If no, what do you need to do to accomplish this?
6. When you block out the voices in your mind that are Not from God, how does that make you feel?
7. What can you do to block the voices of the enemy in your mind where the battle for our Souls is Won?

A is for Adored

Psalm 139:14 "I will give thanks to You, for I am Fearfully and wonderfully made; Wonderful are Your works, and my soul knows that well."

Our Awesome Father God Adores Us! Wow! How Cool is that? Just marvel at the lengths He took to make sure every detail of our being was Unique!

Our Father Loves Us so much that He has Counted every Hair on our head & He has kept all our Tears in a Bottle!

Prayer for Adored,

Awesome Abba, How Wonderful it Feels to be Adored by You! Thank You for making me Fearfully & Wonderful. Please help me to never take this for granted.

I Adore my Private time with You, so Please Keep me Always in Your Grip of Grace.

In the Priceless name of Jesus, Amen.

"His Masterpiece"

We were created to live in Eden, God's true Paradise.

Adam & Eve listened to satan, to their demise? Satan tempted them out of their harmonious unity Stealing their identity & authority.

Sin entered their world with death, sickness, and disease.

Their entire lives were upheaved, they had no peace.

This backlash of sin disgraces our human race.

So brothers & sisters, get on your knees.

Ask God for forgiveness, for your sin to be released.

Priceless is His Peace & His Blessings never cease.

More precious than gold, rubies, all the rare gems.

Come into agreement, as we all say "Amen!" He covers us when others walk away.

Jesus keeps His Promise to us that he will Always Stay!!!

Written by Suzi Weaver.

Questions for the Letter A = Adored

1. Do you know deep in your Heart & Soul you are Adored by God?
2. Do you realize that the Most Important Opinion of you is God's?
3. What Scriptures can you memorize to Know Your True Value & Worth & Treasure you are in God's eyes?
4. How will you Remind yourself of Who God says you are?
5. Once you Understand Your Worth in the Kingdom of Heaven, how will your life change?
6. What will you do to remind yourself daily Who & Whose You are?
7. What will you do to Encourage other women to understand their Value in Christ?

Worship Songs for Lesson #2 Letters B-S:

1. "More than Enough" by Sarah Reeves
2. "Amazing Grace" by Phil Wickman
3. "Diamonds" by Hawk Nelson

B is for Beautiful

Song of Songs 4:7 "You are altogether Beautiful, my darling, there is no flaw in you."

Our Abba sees no flaw in you. He made you, He loves you. You are so Beautiful to Him. He wants you to know how Beautiful you are to Him, no matter what! No matter what you have done or how you see yourself, God, the creator of the Universe, wants you to know How Beautiful you are!

Prayer for Beautiful,

Awesome Abba, help me to understand how You see me. This world can be so cruel, so unkind. I am not of this world because I belong to You! Please remind me when I am not feeling Beautiful how You see me & stand on Your Word!

In the Amazing name of Jesus, Amen.

"Lavishly Loved"

You lavishly loved me right from the start.

You placed my longing for eternity, with You, inside my heart.

You brought into existence all that we see Clearly this is stated in Hebrew 11:3.

Our words frame our world so let us speak life over all.

For this command is from You, who did us all call.

Teach us to expect the Promises in Your Word over our lives.

Declare & receive them with all our might. Goodness, Mercy, Favor, and Grace.

Let these Blessing show upon our Face.

Our Identity is in Christ, not by this fallen place.

I believe what You say about me is True.

Once I was Saved, You made me Brand-New.

You gave us the Fruits of Your Spirit in Galatians 5:22–23.

You gave them to all Your Everyday Girls, just like you gave them to me!

Give us Visions of Compassion to help Save the Lost.

Help us to Bring in Your Harvest, no matter what the Cost!

Written by Suzi Weaver.

Questions for Letter B = Beautiful

1. What words do you say over yourself to remind you of how Beautiful you are in Your Savior's eye?
2. What do you need to do to Believe that you are as Beautiful as God says you are?
3. When you feel Beautiful how do you act?
4. When you don't feel Beautiful how do you act?
5. God looks at Our Hearts. So, do you feel your Heart is Beautiful?
6. If Yes, how so? If No, how so?
7. What can you do Daily to feel Beautiful?

A is for Amazing Grace

Ephesians 1:7 "In Him we have redemption through the blood, the forgiveness of sins, in accordance with the riches of God's grace."

Once we give our life to Christ, He Redeems us with His Amazing Grace. Our sins are forgiven & He Sets Us Free. Who the Son Sets Free is Free Indeed! God's Grace is So Amazing that it is not easy for us to understand. God's Grace is Priceless, so Cherish it.

Prayer for Amazing Grace,

Your Grace is so Amazing to me. Your Grace is a Gift You so Graciously Give to Those who Love You! I would be forever lost without Your Grace. Please continue to remind me of Your Amazing Grace!

In the Unforgettable name of Jesus, Amen.

"Frozen"

Be free, not frozen.

Know that you have been righteously chosen. Declare & believe Jeremiah 29:11.

Spoken over you directly from the throne room of Heaven.

God's plans for our lives are much bigger than you or me. This is His promise, we cannot deny.

Listen to His roar, listen to His thunder.

Women, we were fearlessly made in awe, woven in wonder.

We're not made for this fallen earth,

We're just passing through.

Let Him complete the good works He placed inside of you.

He made you to prosper, increase, and to thrive.

To make you feel, in Him, alive, Not to just barely survive.

So, walk in the way of the Lord with your Holy Spirit guide.

Pleasing fruit you will bear, no more to strive.

Walk in the steps He's guiding you on.

Always chose His kind directions so you won't be wrong.

Reference Scripture Hebrews 1:22.

Confirming He is always looking after you.

Let your heart & mind not be delusional by this fallen world.

Instead, be slayed in the spirit while you dance & you twirl.

Don't get derailed & run off track.

Know that Jesus always will watch your back.

Discover the gifts He sent you to share.

So many are hurting so show them that you care.

Don't go digging up backyard holes that you dug.

Instead, give others your Holy Spirit hug.

Holy Spirit is your greatest teacher, your personally appointed commander chief.

He will fill you with love as opposed to hate from the thief.

Lesson learned is let your critics refine you instead of defining you Cause they're all on the take.

Listening to satan's nasty slimy lying snake.

Jesus has the remedy for all your pain.

You have nothing to lose & everything to gain!

Written by Suzi Weaver.

Questions for Letter A = Amazing

1. What makes you feel Chosen by God?
2. How does it make you feel that God named all the stars in the sky & He felt that world needed your unique self too?
3. How do you explain God's Amazing Grace?
4. How has God's Sweet Grace changed your life?
5. How would you explain God's Grace to your friends or family who aren't Saved yet?
6. What Amazing things has God Blessed your life with lately?
7. How Amazing is His Grace to You?

S is for Shining Light

Matthew 5:14-16 "You are the light of the world. A city set on a hill cannot be hidden."

As a Believer, you have the light of Christ within you to Shine over the darkness of this fallen world. Live as a Shining Light to the Lost, the Hurting, the Lonely, the Confused, and the Hopeless. Your light might be the Only Bright spot in their life so Shine on for Christ to show others His light is available to them too.

Prayer for Shining Light,

Lord, as You light up my life, please help me to light up others as well. You pulled me out of the pit so I could live as Your Shining Light, which I am deeply Grateful for. Use me as Your vessel to Shine Your Light to the Hurting & the Hopeless! In the Brilliant name of Jesus, Amen.

"Diamonds in the Dirt"

Diamonds shine, oh how they shine, Sparkling everywhere.

Shining best on a black background where everyone does stare.

Our diamonds represent the gospel of Jesus displaying brilliant supernatural light.

Sparkling & shining best when placed upon this fallen world's dark evil plight.

So let's go out to sparkle & shine from God's dynamic diamond mine.

To save the lost & lonely before the end of time!

Written by Your Sister in Christ Suzi Weaver.

Questions for Letter S = Shining Light

1. In what way are you Shining your light in this dark world to nudge others toward Jesus?
2. What else can you do to make your light shine even brighter?
3. Where can you or who can you reach who desperately needs your shining light?
4. How do you feel when you shine your light?
5. How do you feel when you don't shine your light?
6. What do you do to make sure your light is always shining on others?
7. What else can you do to brighten other's days with your shining light?

**Worship Songs for Lesson #3
Letters H-E:**

1. "Jesus Cries" by Riley Clemmons
2. "Holy Spirit Come" by Patrick Mayberry
3. "Me on Your Mind" by Anne Wilson & Matthew West

H is for Hope

Jeremiah 29:11 "For I know the plans I have for you, declares the Lord, plans to prosper you and not to harm you, plans to give you Hope and a future."

Isn't it incredible to know that we always have Hope in Christ Jesus! He is our Only Hope. So, whenever life throws you unexpected curve balls just rest assured that your Hope is found in Jesus!

Prayer for Hope,

What an incredible Savior You are that You assured us our Hope can always be found in You! Whenever I feel hopeless, please remind me of Your Promise of Hope for me. In the Hopeful name of Jesus, Amen.

"Choose Me"

I will come running as fast as I can With the Holy Spirit holding my hand.

Into the arms of You Jesus, my father, my friend.

You're inside my Soul, You're my Destiny.

In Your presence, always, is where I long to be.

My greatest treasure is living in Your Glorious Splendor.

For You, my Lord, are my True Pleasure.

Show me Signs & Wonders in Your Heavenly World.

Let me see Amazing Angels in their wind whirling swirls.

Miracles, please let me see.

Your Spiritual Gifts, please give to me.

To help Save the Lost & Lonely, there's no place I'd rather be.

Enlist me into Your Angel Armies, Please Choose Me?

Written by Your Sister in Christ Suzi Weaver.

Questions for Letter H = Hope

1. What is your definition of Hope?
2. How do you feel without Hope?
3. Where is your Hope found?
4. When going through life's storms what do you do to put your Hope in Jesus?
5. What do you do to instill Hope in others?
6. What else can you do to share Hope to others?
7. What do you do to be full of Hope?

E is for Empower

Isaiah 40:31 "They who wait for the Lord shall renew their strength; they shall mount up with wings like eagles; they shall run and not be weary: they shall walk and not faint."

When we are weak God makes us strong. Sometimes we grow weary in this troubled world, but take heart, He who is in us is greater than he who is in this world. Look up to the One who Empowers you.

Prayer for Empowerment,

Amazing Abba Father, Thank You for renewing my strength & Empowering me when I grow weary. You are the Supernatural Energy of Empowerment I need daily, and I give You my gratitude always.

In the Empowering name of Jesus, Amen.

"Clearly"

King of Kings, let me see Clearly. Worshipping & Praying, lest not I tarry? Your Glory is All I Desire to Carry.

Nudging those toward Your Kingdom Who are Lost & Weary? King of Kings let me see Clearly! Open Heaven's gates for Justice to Prevail.

Rip open Your Heavenly Garment, Your Veil.

Make me Brave so Your Story I may Tell.

Helping Others into Heaven, while Saving them from hell.

Oh, King of Kings, let me see Clearly! Crying out to You for all the Injustice Done.

Wash Us clean with Your Waves so all Sin is Gone.

Army Angels are on the Move, Getting into Your Heavenly Groove.

Sweet Jesus, Lifting You Up where You Belong.

Only to Speak Life with Sweet Words Rolling from my Tongue.

King of Kings, Make Me See Clearly!!!

Written by Suzi Weaver.

Questions for Letter E = Empower

1. What Empowers you?
2. What does living Empowered look like for you?
3. What do you do to stay Empowered?
4. Who/What is your Confidence in?
5. What are you doing to help Empower others?
6. What else can you do to help Empower others?
7. What would your life look like without Empowerment?

Worship Songs for Lesson #4 Letters D-Y:

1. "Holy Water" by We the Kingdom
2. "No Stranger" by Natalie Grant
3. "Take it All Back" by Tauren Wells

D is for Divine

Romans 1:20 "For since the creation of this world His invisible attributes, His eternal power and Divine nature, have been clearly seen, being understood through what has been made, so they are without excuse."

Everywhere you look you can see the Divine Nature of God. From spectacular sunsets to wonderful waterfalls, from precious babies to adorable animals, His Divine creation is put on splendor just for us. Appreciate all that He puts on display which is so Divine.

Prayer for Divine,

Artist Abba, Your Divine nature astounds me with its beauty & wonder. Thank You for painting our world with such beauty & grace. Help me to always appreciate Your Divine nature, just for me. In the Divine name of Jesus, Amen.

"Purposely Passionate"

Be purposely passionate for Our King to come.
Heaven invading earth until His will is done.
Protection we need from His Spiritual realm.
Worship, Praise Him till your Soul is calm.
Hunger for His anointing oil to fall over you.
Jesus, your first love, He will to you be true.
Keep Him, Always, at the top of your list.
So, Blessings from Him will never be missed.
Fill yourself daily with His Holy Grace.
Shining His Glory all over your face.
His Promises, do not displace.
Shine His light to Save the Lost.
Align with Jesus, no matter what the cost.
Written by Sister Suzi.

Questions for the Letter D = Divine:

1. What does the word Divine mean to you?
2. Who/What is Divine to you?
3. What is the Divine nature of the Trinity?
4. How Divine do you feel when you are in the very Presence of Our Divine Creator?
5. Divinely speaking, what Scriptures reinforce to you the Divinity?
6. When witnessing to others how would you explain Our Divine Creator to unbelievers?
7. What in your life is Divine to you?

L is for Loved

John 3:16 "For this is how God loved the world: He gave us His one and only Son, so that everyone who believes in Him will not perish but have everlasting life."

Jesus Loved us enough to die for us, just let that sink in. God didn't want to live without us, so He brought Heaven here! That's how much we are Loved by Our Heavenly Father! Wow!

Prayer for Loved,

Abba Father God, You gave Your life so that I might have eternity with You. I can only imagine how deep Your Love is for me. What a glorious Promise to spend eternity with You! Please remind me how much You Love me when I feel unloved.

In the Loving name of Jesus, Amen.

"He Chose the Nails"

I love because I've been set free, my bondage is no more. Jesus touched my heart with love, my chains fell to the floor.

I prayed His light would saturate my heart of stone & pain.

He washed me with His blood so red, it came like heavy rain.

When the unexpected comes & life seems hard to bare, Release Your Heart to Jesus Christ, it only takes a prayer. His sacrifice upon the cross was bound by love, not nails.

The Matchless One that we can trust, JESUS NEVER FAILS!

Written by Beverly Jo Gerlitz.

Questions for the Letter L = Loved

1. Do you know the depths of God's Love for you?
2. How does His sacrifice of having His Only Son be Ransomed for your sins feel?
3. Jesus Loves You, in fact He thought you were to die for!
4. How can you fathom that kind of Love?
5. When you don't feel Loved what can you do to remind yourself that you are?
6. How do you share God's Love with others?
7. What else can you do to share God's Love to a hurting world?

Y is for Yes to Abba Father God, Sweet Son Jesus, and Hovering Holy Spirit

Romans 10:9-10 "If you confess with your mouth that Jesus is Lord and believe in your heart that God raised Him from the dead, you will be saved. For with the heart, one believes and is justified, and with the mouth one confesses and is saved."

What a Gracious Gift from God for our salvation. Once we let Him into our mind, heart, and soul our life will never be the same. Our Savior Saves!

Prayer for Yes,

A thousand times Yes, I surrender my life to You! Abba Father, Thank You for Saving my Soul & claiming it for Your own. Thank You for Saving me from darkness & bringing me into Your marvelous light. Forever I will Praise Your Holy name.

In the Saving name of Jesus, Amen.

"Jesus Joy"

A life in Christ I choose to live.

He only abundantly life does give.

Jesus is the lover of my soul.

My story now, it must be told.

He sends His angels like the wind with burning flames of fire.

Ask for His angelic help to take you into the spiritual realm higher.

As stated in Hebrews 1:7 & Psalms 91:11

He commands His angels to guard & protect you in all your ways.

Scripture backs this up, just look at Matthew 4:11 & Psalm 103:20 & Acts 10:3.

It's in His word, the truth for all to see.

Supernatural gifts can really get you going to open that angelic door.

It states this clearly in Luke Chapter 4!

If you want angelic encounters then be devoted in your prayers.

Blessings abound on all God's daughters & sons, all us rightful heirs!

Poem written by Suzi Weaver.

Questions for the Letter Y = Yes to Abba Father God, Sweet Son Jesus and Hovering Holy Spirit:

1. Have you given your life to Christ?
2. If not, when?
3. If so, how did that Choice make you feel then?
4. Since accepting Christ as your Savior, how do you feel about that Choice now?
5. Have you been baptized?
6. If not, when?
7. If so, how did that Choice make you feen then & now?

**Worship Songs for Lesson #5
Letters B-O:**

1. "Trample" by Kim Walker Smith
2. "Hosanna" by Brooke Ligertwood
3. "The Break Up Song" by Francesca Battistelli

B is for Bold

Proverbs 28:1 "The wicked flee when no one pursues, but the righteous are Bold as a lion."

Be Bold as the Lion of Judah! Your confidence comes from the Lord Himself. Stand Up for those who can't defend themselves. They need your Bold faith to help them, protect them, and share God's love for them!

Prayer for Bold,

Abba Father, make me Bold as the Lion of Judah as I walk through this life. Please help me to Boldly rescue others from the devil's demise & Boldy share Your Love with them so they may be Saved!

In the Bold name of Jesus, Amen.

"Kick Up Some Dust"

The Trinity is made up of Three in One; God the Father, Holy Spirit, and Jesus the Son.

Our Battles They've Already Won.

On the Cross it was Finished, It's Over, It's Done! Humanity in the Palm of His Hands Begun.

Our Fight is Not with Flesh & Blood.

Holy Spirit Invade Us, Our Atmosphere Flood.

Angel Armies on the Rise.

So, the Lost will be Found In a True Believers Eyes.

One Million Soul Harvest in 2020 Prophesized. Bring it on, Let's Kick up some Dust.

Showing Others how to Follow Jesus is the Only Life for Us!!!

Written by Suzi Weaver.

Questions for the Letter B = Bold

1. What makes you feel Bold, like the Lion of Judah?
2. What actions do you display when you feel Bold?
3. Do you share your Boldly faith?
4. If not, why?
5. If so, how?
6. What can you do to motivate yourself to act Bold?
7. What can you do to share how to be Bold with others?

O is for Opportunity

Galatians 6:10 "So then, as we have Opportunity, let us do good to everyone, and especially to those who are of the household of faith."

Seize every opportunity each day brings for God. Opportunities will be all round you, so whether God has placed someone on your heart today or given you an assignment for someone, or set you up with a divine appointment, use all these Opportunities to Share His Love with others.

Prayer for Opportunity,

Gracious God, Thank You for every single Opportunity You send my way to share Your Word. I gratefully receive all requests from You to Witness to others however You ask me to, so You receive all the Glory.

In the Matchless name of Jesus, Amen.

"Our Invitation"

Our invitation to the table is accepted by our Faith, Gather others, to the table bring.

So, they can come to know Our Glorious King.

Metaphorically speaking He named these lost to find.

Our Savior did this for us all, He is so very kind.

Bring to me the poor, the crippled, blind & lame.

Hosanna in the Highest, He is calling out your name.

Read in Mark 11:1-11 Proclaiming what will be sent from Heaven.

To this table I've prepared to be your Gracious Host.

Spared by Our Father, only through me, so that no one can boast.

Take off your cloaks of bondage to release your pain.

You will then be delivered as Jesus does break your chains.

For the Son of man came to seek & save the lost, No matter what the cost.

Jesus saved us when we were broken, not at our best.

So that we will seek out others, so let's go find the rest.

It states in Luke 19:10, Jesus healed with a victorious amen.

On Good Friday it was finished, His victory was won.

Redeeming Souls is what He does, so get out there & move along.

When He rides upon that white horse named Faithful & True.

He is riding down from Heaven to come back just for You!

Written by Suzi Weaver.

Questions for the Letter
O = Opportunity

1. What does Opportunity mean to you?
2. What Opportunities have you embraced to live for Christ?
3. What other Opportunities can you find to live for Christ?
4. What Opportunities has God blessed you with recently for your life?
5. What Opportunities are you looking for in your life?
6. What can you do to bless others with the Opportunities you have been given?
7. Who else can you partner with as an Opportunity to bless others?

Worship Songs for Lesson #6 Letters L-D:

1. "There was Jesus" by Zach Williams & Dolly Parton
2. "Rise Up" by Cain
3. "Come Jesus Come" by Stephen McWhirter

L is for Lean on Christ

Proverbs 3:5 "Trust in the Lord with all your heart, and do not lean on your own understanding."

As we Lean into Christ He directs our path. His ways are higher than our ways, so, trust in Him. Stay in His Word & listen to His Whisper anytime you need direction & He will set your path straight.

Prayer for Lean on Christ,

Christ Jesus, I am so ecstatic to know I can Lean on You anytime, anywhere, anyplace, and You will set me on the right course for my life & my destiny. Please correct me when I get off course & help me to listen to Your gentle whisper as I Lean on You.

In the Matchless name of Jesus, Amen.

"Our Rock"

On Christ the Solid Rock we Stand.

All other Ground is Sinking Sand.

We know the end is Near to Come, Into Heaven's Gates we will Run.

Until then we Must Stand Strong In the Face of Evil & All Wrong.

His Perfect Love Casts out All Fear.

So, Keep Him in Your Heart So Dear.

Always Stay by Jesus Side.

In His Truth You will Abide.

When Your Storms are Raging High Look Up to Jesus in the Sky.

He will comfort You with His Peace.

Bringing Sighs of Sweet Release.

In His Grip You must Remain.

For His Love Always Stays the Same.

On Christ the Solid Rock we Stand.

All other ground is Sinking Sand!

Written by Suzi Weaver Inspired by her Sister Bev.

Questions for the Letter L = Lean on Christ

1. What does Leaning on Christ mean to you?
2. When do you Lean on Christ & what do you do?
3. What does your life look like when you don't lean on Christ?
4. How is that working for you?
5. What other ways can you Lean on Christ?
6. How can you share with others how to Lean on Christ?
7. Who else will help you?

D is for Dance

Ecclesiastes 3:4 "A time to weep and a time to laugh: A time to mourn and a time to dance."

Dance, dance, dance. It's time for you to Dance! Dancing is such a joyous activity; it just makes your Soul sing! There might be weeping in the night, however, God Promises you there will be Joy in the morning. So, I choose to start off every day listening to Worship & Dancing!

Prayer for Dance,

Amazing Abba, Thank You for giving me the ability to Dance, even when life's storms come my way. Please help me to remember to always Dance in the rain! In the Musical name of Jesus, Amen.

"Dance"

You have Waited so long to feel His Sweet Release.

Now it's Your turn for His Sounds, in Your Life, to be Unleashed.

Dance to His Music as You Reach for the Stars.

They're Closer to You than You Know, Not Far.

Joy out of Your Ashes, It's Your turn to Shine.

Beautiful Beverly Jo, Amazing Sister of Mine!

Written by Your Admiring Sister Suzi.

Questions for the Letter D = Dance

1. Do you Dance often?
2. If not, why?
3. If yes, when & to what kind of music?
4. How does Dancing make you feel?
5. What do you need to change in your life so you Dance more?
6. What motivated you to Dance?
7. Dancing is a celebration, so when are you going to go Dance in the rain?

Worship Songs for Lesson #7 Conclusion:

1. "Lion of Judah" by Chris Brown & Brandon Lake
2. "Run to the Father" by Kari Jobe & Cody Carnes
3. "I Can Only Imagine" by Mercy Me

"Whispers"

She was bound by shame & shackled

While the demon witches cackled.

She could see them dancing in his eyes.

Then Jesus whispered to her "My Darling Daughter, don't listen to their lies."

She felt like she was going crazy, that insanity was approaching way too fast.

Then Jesus whispered to her "My Darling Daughter, You are of sound mind & this won't last."

She felt strange suffocation wrapped around her like that of a lethal python snake.

Then Jesus whispered to her "My Darling Daughter, all of Your pain I will gladly take."

She then was being silently tormented by a muzzle strapped tightly across her face.

Then Jesus whispered to her "My Darling Daughter, You belong with Me, You'll always have a place."

As she cried out to Him broken & forsaken.

Then Jesus whispered to her "My Darling Daughter, Your Soul I've claimed, it's already taken."

Lord, please tell me what's going on, either that, or just let me die?

Then Jesus whispered to her "My Darling Daughter, If You would only seek Me, at least give Me a try."

"Show me Lord," she shouted "What is happening?"

Then Jesus whispered to her "My Darling Daughter, Ephesians 6:12 to you I bring."

Tears of deep compassion started streaming down her cheeks.

Then Jesus whispered to her "My Darling Daughter, I will make You strong when you feel weak."

He delivered her from the darkness, He delivered her from the pit.

Then Jesus whispered to her "My Precious Daughter, Only with Me is where You truly fit!"

In remembrance of the very day she was Saved by her Savior, which was on November 4, 2004. Written by His Grateful Daughter, Suzi Weaver on August 4, 2019. Finished at exactly 11:11 a.m.

Invitation Prayer to Open Your Heart to Jesus.....

Abba Father, Sweet Son Jesus, Hovering Holy Spirit, I Open My Heart to You Today!

I Believe You are My Creator, that Jesus Died on the Cross Carrying Our Sins, Guilt, & Shame. I Believe Jesus Rose Again on the Third Day while Conquering Death, the Grave, and the Grip of satan on My Life!

Please Forgive Me for All of My Sins & Transgressions that I or Anyone in My Bloodline has Ever Committed Against You!

I Come to You Just as I am. I Receive Your Gift of Grace Over My Life Now in the Precious, Priceless, Powerful Name of Jesus! Amen!

www.ingramcontent.com/pod-product-compliance
Lightning Source LLC
Chambersburg PA
CBHW052125070526
44586CB00016B/2082